> *"Treat yourself with love and respect and you will attract people who show you love and respect."*
>
>
> The Secret

*There comes a time in your life where you have to
ask yourself: when is enough, enough?
How much longer will you choose*

suffering over joy, pain over triumph,
*fear over the exhilaration of living life to its fullest?
You can have everything you want, you just have to move forward.*

Are you ready?
Is enough finally enough?

You're officially taking the first step.

Part of creating a wonderful life for yourself lies in **gratitude**. The more grateful you are for what you have, the more things appear for you to be grateful for.

Try starting your day by listing what you're grateful for—friends, family, pets, things you're able to do, places you can go…. If you constantly live in a mindset of lacking, you'll always be lacking. **Change** your perspective to one that celebrates what you have and

N. Y.

M

you will learn how truly blessed you are.

WHAT ARE YOUR DREAMS?

Are you ready to see them realized? First, you have to identify everything you'd like to accomplish over the next year in every aspect of your life—health, career, romance. Make a list of it and post it somewhere you will see everyday. Spend some time focusing on your list, and imagine that it has already come true. You will begin your new life path the best way by visualizing what you want and imagining the feeling of achieving it. You have to believe in your dreams and in your power to make them a reality.

Wednesday

Whether you're thinking positively or negatively, the universe will deliver whatever it is that's in your brain. Knowing that, wouldn't you rather choose positive thoughts? That's the best way to ensure your happy ending.

Thursday

Today, understand this one principle:

You are the giant magnet that can attract positive energy or negative energy.
A person is the product of his thoughts and becomes what he thinks.
The only way to attract positive energy is to put out positive energy.
Have you ever noticed that it is much easier to be friendly than it is to be mean?
Do positive actions in order for the universe to be in your favor.

Friday

Life is about choice. You may not be able to control the weather or the emotions of others, but you can control your emotions and your reactions. Make the choice today to have a positive outlook on life—no matter if it rains all day and you've planned a picnic or forgotten your umbrella. The more you train yourself to think positively, the more you will clear any obstacle from leading the life that you want to live.

Changing your thought
patterns can be a challenge,

Saturday

but it's possible—it's just a matter of choice. Negative thoughts will come into your mind, but you don't have to accept them. Just change your mind and think of the exact opposite. With practice, your mind will start doing that on its own.

Sunday

Sometimes, it's hard to change our mindset when we're doing the same things in the same places, day in and day out. Today, challenge your routine and take yourself out of your comfort zone. Maybe have something different for lunch, take an alternate route to work, or talk to someone you've never spoken to before.

You never know what simple experiences like this can reveal to you.

The next time
you're tempted
to complain,
stop. Take a
moment, look at
the situation,
and try to *find*
the good in what's
happening—
no matter how
minute the good
may seem. The
more you seek out
the positive, the
more it will
come to you.
Focusing on the
negative will
only bring you
more of it.

Don't let your negative thoughts scare you.

Although you want to focus on the positive as much as possible, having a negative thought isn't going to throw you off track. Sometimes negative thoughts can act as our warning signs or red flags in certain situations. It is up to you to determine whether you need to be more cautious or more positive. But always keep in mind that substituting negative thoughts with simple caution is hundreds of times more powerful than thinking negatively.

Wednesday

Remember, you are a magnet—so what is it you want to attract to yourself? Instead of saying what you don't want to happen, start saying what you do want to *happen*. Then, reiterate it both out loud and in your head as much as you feel comfortable with. Soon, it will become *natural*. Before you know it, it will be in *your life*.

Thursday

When you visualize your goals, what do you feel?
Are you *passionate* about them, or does it not matter
if you achieve them or not?

When you're *passionate* about something, the universe responds.
When you're ambivalent toward something, the universe responds.
Keep that in mind when setting your goals for the future.

You may want everything you desire to happen for you right here and now, but the universe just doesn't work that way. There's a time delay that exists between your visualization and your goal's achievement, just make sure that it's what you really want.

This is why it's so important to choose positively over negatively— your thoughts compound over time. Wouldn't you rather they be good ones?

Friday

Saturday

Is there something you haven't asked for because of your fear it won't come true? *Doubt is a powerful thing*, but doubt will never be as *powerful as positive thinking*. Understand that even if you can't believe right away, you can always just ask right away, and then act positively. Assure yourself that everything you do positively puts money in the positive bank and allows you to build on your belief.

It is through positive thinking that you gain what you want. *Believe in the positive* and you will begin to get the things for which you ask.

Sunday

Take time to evaluate your life, and when you do, look at the glass as half full, not half empty, look at all you have rather than what you don't have. You have to let go of your negative thoughts and actively replace them with positive ones. Once you begin this practice, all else will follow.

Monday

It's not enough to believe and see what your heart desires—you have to pay attention to the signs.

Are your eyes and mind wide open?

Realize that even the worst life experiences have a gem wrapped inside them. Though it may not seem it at the time, not getting that particular job, being late for an appointment, even a nonsensical dream or odd saying that catches your ear can be a guide to the path you're supposed to take.

Tuesday

Part of achieving your dreams is identifying old thought patterns and demolishing them to make way for bigger, better and faster thoughts dedicated to creating the life you want to live. Tune into your subconscious and try meditating to help clear out the old mental clutter. Start by sitting quietly, maybe for 10 minutes a day, and work up to a time that feels comfortable for you. You'll be amazed at the changes you'll see and feel, mentally and physically.

Wednesday

Try writing them down to get them out of your head, then write the antithesis or solution to them on another page. Then, focus on the solutions and positives rather than the things that are holding you back. The simple act of addressing your fears can take the power away from them and turn them into motivators.

Being far away from your goals can sometimes make you feel hopeless. In that case, get as close to them as you can. Do you want a big house? Drive through ritzy neighborhoods and admire the homes you like, imagining yourself in one of them. A cool sports car? Why not go for a test drive? Rich and everlasting love? Watch for couples canoodling in the park, and imagine what they're feeling.

Thursday

One day, you'll be able to set an example for someone else.

Friday

Do you know where
your thoughts are going?
When you feel your
brain going off on a
tangent, follow it—see
where it leads you. Is it
thinking about good,
positive things, or is it
rehashing the negatives
of your past and pres-
ent? When you identify
where the chain of
events starts, it becomes
easier to identify your
negative triggers.

Setbacks are a part of life—not everything goes exactly the way we want, but everything is a part of a bigger plan for us. When things seem to not be going your way, know and trust that the universe is conspiring—along with your actions—to bring you exactly what you desire, but often administers tests to see if you're ready. The reward is never as sweet when it's easily gained. Remember that as you're weathering the storm.

Saturday

Don't lose hope.

Sunday

Nobody said changing your life would be easy. In fact, it hurts the most when you're growing because you're expanding so that you're prepared to accept more good in your life. When all hope seems lost, go back to a time when you felt like you had it all and relive that feeling—it will happen again if you believe.

Remember—out of the greatest despairs come the greatest gifts.

Holding back your happiness can actually rob others from learning valuable lessons, and can actually impede your growth. If you're enjoying life, why not share it? Not only will it be infectious, but it will help reaffirm your position and attract more positive things to you.

*When you are focusing on things you want to attract into
your life, it's important that you feel good—feeling good is
what is going to help bring your dreams to fruition.*

Tuesday

*Take time out to pamper yourself, whether that means a day at the spa or sleeping in.
It's all about what you feel inside, and when you feel good, good things happen.*

It's time to take action. While wishing is part of the equation, you have to make positive steps toward achieving your dreams, no matter how small those steps seem. Do you want a house overlooking the ocean in Hawaii? Start researching areas you're interested in, and familiarize yourself with the lay of the land.

Wednesday

Looking for that perfect partner? Start expanding your circle of friends and go to new places, try new things. Every step you take in the name of achieving your dreams is a step forward.

Whose life do you want to emulate if you had the choice? If there's someone whose life path you admire, focus on them when you meditate and draw in their energy. Post pictures of them in places where you can see them.

Thursday

Use their image to help inspire you to stay on your path.

Friday

Placing an order with the universe is like placing an order at a restaurant—you look at a menu and decide what you want, then you take the steps to ensure you acquire it. To speed things up, why not create a menu? Take pictures that represent what you want out of magazines and make a collage of it, then place it somewhere you'll see it every day. Meditate on it. Rest your eyes on it when you're blue. Then, pay attention to how you feel when you look at it.

IT'S ALL PART OF THE PROCESS.

Saturday

If you think your wants and desires are too far out of reach, stop and reflect on some of the incredible things people have achieved all over the world. We've built spaceships and landed on the moon, we've run marathons, we've created machines to fly all over the world, we've made incredible things happen every day.

This is proof that if you really want it, it can happen.

Don't let go of your goals and dreams,
no matter how out of reach they seem.

Sunday

The minute you do, they start to slip away and disappear, taking you further and further from the life you want to live. Instead, when the road seems darkest, focus more. Visualize more. Plan and wish more. It's just the universe testing you to see if that's what you really want.

The mind is a powerful tool, and we often don't think about how it helps create our life. If you want a sign that you've got the power, just ask for one. Start your day with a general idea of how you'd like it to turn out, then ask for a sign from the universe that it's listening. You might be surprised at what you find.

Tuesday

When you envision your *life's desire*, do you see it with your head or with your heart? Sometimes your mind can cause negative chattering to discourage your life pursuits— and can often argue with "logic" against what your ultimate goals are, whereas your heart is unencumbered by such programming. Seeing your path with your heart instead of your mind connects it to your very soul, bringing it all the more into *focus*.

Notes

*"Success is focusing the
full power of all you are on
what you have a burning
desire to achieve"*

Wilfred Peterson

If you can see it in your mind, you can hold it in your hand, so to speak… so why not turn your brain into your own movie theater? Project the life you want to live in the theater of your mind, and allow yourself to get immersed in the experience.

Pretending

to live it, be it, feel it is a great way to get used to having it. By the time it arrives, you'll be well prepared.

*How fast you achieve your dreams depends on how **hard** you're working to achieve them. Are you sitting on your sofa dreaming about what you want, or are you visualizing, paying attention to the signs, and taking steps in the direction of where you want to be? Wishing is part of it, but acting in ways that bring your goals into* **focus** *help them become more real.*

What have you done today to bring yourself one step closer to where you want to be?

The Law of Attraction states that the images in your mind draw things to you, whether you like it or not. What are you attracting into your life? Take a moment to examine what you think about when you awake, check in during the day, and take stock again at night. When you're breaking negative habits, the negative chatter in your mind will always fight back.

YOU CAN TAME IT.

Saturday

When you notice yourself surrounded with a lot of negativity and anger despite all your hard work, it's time to sit up and pay attention. What is it that you're not seeing? What is the universe trying to tell you? Take a moment to step outside of yourself to help understand why you are where you are. Then, you can get back on the path.

Sunday

Do you pay attention to how you feel when you speak?

If you're speaking from a place of contentedness and love, contentment and love will follow. If you're speaking from a place of pain or anger, guess what? When you're tempted to speak ill, stop yourself and see if you can say good instead of evil.

When you understand where you are versus where you want to be, you create a clearer path to achieving your goals than if you haphazardly throw everything to the wind. Make sure you clearly define your goals and pay attention to the signs that will lead you there, or else you'll forever be on the wrong path.

Take a look at the greatest, most accomplished people throughout history,

and you'll find a common thread—their path wasn't easy, but it was worth it. When you're struggling to see the light, do some research on some of the great people who made an impact in this world, and use their struggles as lessons to help you get through.

Wednesday

There's a difference between desire and desperation. Desire comes from a concrete want and a feeling that you truly deserve something, whereas desperation comes from a feeling of lack and need. Make sure you analyze the depths of where your goals are coming from, and ensure you're sending the right message into the universe.

Otherwise, you might not like what you get.

Being in the depths
of despair is never
fun, and sometimes
it still *happens*
despite our best
efforts. Instead of
wallowing in it, dig
deep and find the
strength to think
about how much
better life will
be when you're
out of your sad
situation. It takes
practice, but
soon you'll
discover life is
easier to navigate
without the weight
of the world on
your shoulders.

Paying attention to what you feel

like when you get up in the morning can help you determine your day. If you had a bad dream, write it down and get it out of your head so you can focus on having a better day. If you woke up feeling wonderful, focus on that and continue to build on it no matter what comes your way. Doing that will help ensure you have more good days than bad!

Saturday

When someone asks you how you are, what do you say? Do you tell them "Not bad," or do you say, "I'm good"? The more you affirm the positive in your life, the more the positive will affirm you. Soon, you'll be telling people you're *fantastic*, **stupendous** *and* **wonderful!**

Sunday

Miracles happen every day—you just have to know how to look for them. Most people expect miracles to be huge events. Sometimes they are, but other times they're subtle and simple.

Today, look back on your life and see if you can spot the *miracles*. Then, invite more to come along.

Your life can change in the blink of an eye. One minute can be full of despair and hopelessness, but all that can change with a phone call or an e-mail.

You're entitled to miracles— especially when you know that you deserve them. Treat yourself as though you deserve a miracle every day...which is a miracle in itself.

Monday

Tuesday

Do you feel yourself surrounded by *love, prosperity, and good health?*
Part of the process is enjoying and reveling in the feeling of what it's like to have
what you want, so take a moment to close your eyes and *immerse yourself*
in the feeling of unconditional love, infinite prosperity, and living in a
strong, healthy body. Even if you've never had those things before, you'll be
amazed at how *easy* it is to imagine them.

WHEN YOU BEGIN TO UNDERSTAND

that every aspect of life is a gift, you start to understand that there are good things in every situation. Today, take time out to be appreciative of the gifts life has given you, even if it's as simple as a cloudless day or clean socks. It'll make those tougher days easier to deal with.

Thursday

Does attaining your goals feel like too much work?
Maybe you're not having enough fun with the process! Immerse yourself in the joy of anticipating the gifts you'll be given, almost as if you're a kid at Christmas. It will help you feel good when it seems there's no end in sight.

Friday

Sometimes, feeling empowered is just a matter of choosing the right words to help guide you in your life. Words like "Fear," "Anger" and "Hate" feel scary and sad, while words like "Gratitude," "Happiness" and "Love" feel wonderful and light. Make a list of the words that make you happy, and remind yourself of them every day—twice a day on the days you feel the most darkness.

If one bad experience is leading into another that leads into another, find the power to make it stop. Analyze the situation and see where it started so you can understand how to avoid it in the future, then start making positive changes to get you moving in the right direction.

It's all about staying on your path.

Are there people in your life that you just don't click with? Rather than looking at them as a burden, try to understand why they're there. Perhaps they're teaching you a lesson, acting as a bridge to something that will bring you closer to your goal, showing you how far you've come, or maybe they're acting as a mirror, giving you a perspective on yourself that you've never seen.

Sunday

They're there for a reason—it's just a matter of which one.

Having a bad day at work? Is traffic making you crazy? Maybe someone you know is causing you stress. Whatever it is, you have the power to change how it makes you feel. Just picture something you love in your mind, and focus on it—it could be a friend, your pet, a place you like to vacation…whatever it is, see it in your mind's eye and feel the happiness that comes along with it. Whatever was bothering you will disappear like water off a duck's back.

We're always tempted to find the bad in people, because finding the bad is easy—everyone has negative traits. Why not try to find the good ones instead? When we look for the good in people, it helps us see them in a new light and gives us new options. Plus, the more positivity you find and appreciate, the more you'll attract.

Tuesday

Recognize that everyone in your life is a mirror—what you dislike in others is actually what you dislike in yourself. Instead of criticizing the shortcomings of others, focus on improving your own.

It's amazing the wonderful people you attract into your life that way.

If you're having trouble with a friend or loved one, change your perspective of them by writing down one thing every day that you like about them for a month. At the end of that month, review the list. It'll serve as a helpful reminder of why they're in your life. Can't come up with anything? Maybe it's time to move on.

Our problem with relationships—be they friendships, working relationships or romantic relationships—is we're constantly focusing on what the other person does wrong instead of what they do right. Guess what?

Friday

That just emphasizes the bad. Look for the good in others, and praise them for the good that they are. You just might find more of that good stuff coming your way.

*Know that there is enough abundance for everyone, but if you act in ways that
deplete others of their goals and desires, it will come back to haunt you.
Today, ensure that you're being as generous in helping others toward their goals
as you are to yourself and it will come back to you tenfold.*

Saturday

If you're worried, in fear, or thinking about the worst that could happen, you can't be surprised when that's what you're handed in life. Though it's not easy, choosing to have the opposite feeling—no matter the situation—helps to bring you out of that downward spiral.

Today, pay attention to when you feel those negative emotions, and see what you can do to change things around. If you've done all you can, that's all you can do…so don't dwell on things.

Sunday

Instead, do something that makes you happy.

You have more control over things than you think you do—especially when life feels like it's a runaway train. Only you can slow that train down, so take time today to figure out where the chaos is in your life, and discover how to calm it. Maybe it means taking more time out for yourself, turning off the TV, spending time with people who nurture you.

These simple changes can bring about a world of good.

Tuesday

Music can have an incredible influence on your mood. It has the power to lift you up or bring you down, all with the power of words and melody. If you're trying to bring yourself out of a sad situation, put on your favorite happy songs and throw yourself into the joy of them. Your mood will change in no time,

and you'll be back to your positive, attractive self.

Feeling chained is never fun, so why not break free?

Wednesday

The only thing that's holding you back from doing what you want to do is you! Quit that job you hate and find one you love, express yourself openly and honestly, run naked into the ocean…do whatever it is you want to do that's within your reach while you're working on achieving your goals. Every step towards happiness helps.

Notes

"You are never given a wish without also being given the power to make it true. You may have to work for it, however."

Richard Bach

You may not have the car you want, the house you want, the relationship you want or the body you want, but focusing on that—or looking at someone who has less and putting yourself above them—just blocks you from what you really do want. Make sure to focus on what you have and want, not you lack.

If you have trouble feeling gratitude for what you have, find something you can designate as a reminder so that every time you look at it, you remember to feel *grateful* for what you have in life. It could be a ribbon, a rock or maybe a picture hanging on your wall. Whatever it is, make sure you set your intention to have it remind you. It will make feelings of *gratitude* instantaneous.

Feel like your mind and thoughts are **separate** *from you?*
There's one simple way to bring it all into focus—
pay attention *to your feelings.*

If you sense yourself getting furious, or feel the tinglings of joy, take a moment to live in the moment and decide if that's where you really want to be.

Soon, your body and mind will be one.

*Everything positive you attract into your life brings you one step closer to your **goal**, whether it's a book, a person, a plant…anything!*
Pay attention *to what's coming to you and how it correlates with what your goals are.*

N. Y.

You'll be surprised at what can help you get to where you want to go.

Have you ever thought about someone and they call or e-mail you the next day? That's the Law of Attraction at work. See what else you can attract into your life just by thinking about it. It's amazing what can happen when you set your mind to it.

One of the simplest ways to start creating the life that you want is to script it out.
Sit down and start writing about what your life is going to be like, and notice the feelings
it stirs in you. Tune in to that frequency, and the universe will respond.

Wednesday

Don't let your mind get in the way of your goals,

*no matter how unreachable they might seem—let the universe
worry about how to bring what you want to you. Instead, dream big.
Dream without borders, restrictions and restraints. Let your imagination go wild.
Wouldn't you rather see what it's like to have it all than to doubt having it all?*

Thursday

You may not know how your goals and dreams are going to come true, but that's because you're trying to live in the future. Live in the present, and the pathway to achieving those goals and dreams will be revealed to you. You don't have to know how it's going to happen, you just have to know that it will. Everything else will fall into place.

The minute you start to
doubt your goals and dreams,

Friday

the universe responds in kind. To that end, you want to ensure that you not only believe that you deserve everything you want, but that you can have it, too. The minute you start to doubt, it starts to disappear.

Saturday

The definition of insanity is repeatedly approaching the same situation with the same behaviors and expecting a different result every time. If you find yourself caught in a loop,

it means there's a lesson you're not learning—and that's moving you farther and farther away from where you want to be.

When you change your perspective on a situation, you change your life.

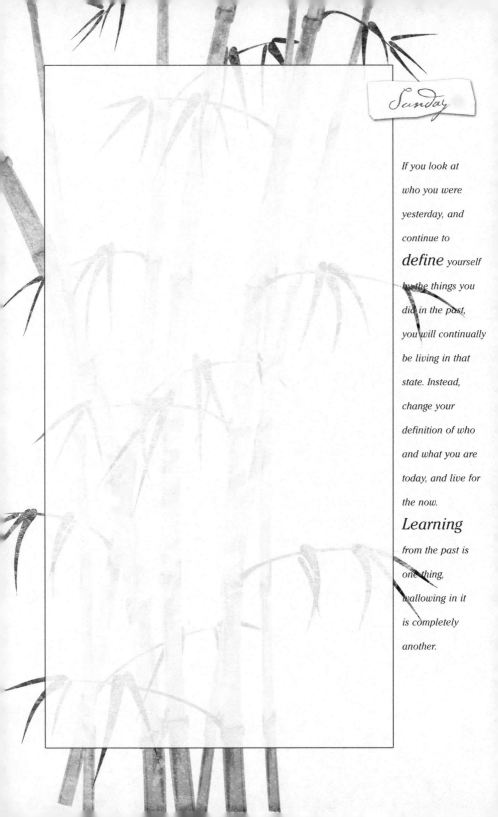

Sunday

If you look at who you were yesterday, and continue to **define** *yourself by the things you did in the past, you will continually be living in that state. Instead, change your definition of who and what you are today, and live for the now.* **Learning** *from the past is one thing, wallowing in it is completely another.*

Part of getting what you want lies within you.

Listen to your instinct – it always knows the answer. Before you make a decision on something, check in with yourself and see what your intuition says. It's never wrong.

Tuesday

It's not enough to *know* and *see* what you want—you have to set your intention on it. That means that every day you have to know, feel and believe with every bone in your body that what you want is what you *deserve*, without fear, without doubt. Make your intention *strong*.

Wednesday

Setting your *intention* to achieve your goals will bring inspiration from the strangest places. The important thing is not to question it—just go for it when you really know it's right.

People will drop into your life, ideas will pop into your head, and doors will open at random, all with the common theme of taking you toward your goal. *Go for it!*

Manifesting your dreams into reality is a process, and it starts simply. If you're skeptical about making things happen, begin with little things and work your way up. It could be as simple as wanting a good parking spot, an easy day at work, or the person you like in your office to say hello to you in the morning.

When you start to see things happening, you'll be motivated to have bigger and better dreams and goals.

Thursday

Friday

If you're really manifesting your **dreams and goals**, *it's going to feel fabulous. If you feel like you're struggling and not achieving anything, you're not on the right path. Analyze your actions every step of the way to ensure the moves you're making make you happy. That's when you know that* **life** *is giving you what you want.*

Saturday

Working toward your dreams and goals should never be a chore. If it is, you've either deviated from the plan, or your desires and goals have changed. Today, examine how it makes you feel to think about what you want. If you're feeling negatively about it, change your course.

YOU'RE NEVER STUCK WHERE YOU ARE.

Sunday

Using mantras is a powerful tool for helping change where you are. Want more money? Try reciting, "Money comes easily, effortlessly and frequently" to yourself in the mirror every morning. How about love? Say, "I want and deserve a love that is whole, encompassing and fulfilling." Look at your reflection and tell it what you want.

This is one of the most powerful ways to set your intention.

Living in joy is about living in possibility, which creates hope and opportunities for greatness. How are you living in joy? Make a list and see how you can expand it.

Instead of looking for the major milestones in life, start by celebrating the small ones. Getting to work on time, having a delicious cup of coffee, a gloriously sunny day…all of these things are cause for celebration.

And remember—the more you celebrate,

the more good things come your way.

Once you've asked, it listens. All you have to do is keep taking the steps you need to in order to bring it to fruition. If you're begging, you're in a repetitive process and you're not moving forward. Make sure that you're always heading toward your goal, not merely treading water.

You don't need to repeatedly ask the universe to grant your desires.

Thursday

Part of making your
dreams come true
includes trusting in
the universe to hear
your request and
take care of it. When
you've meditated on
and visualized what
you want for the day,
set your intention to
release it to the
universe and leave it
in its capable hands.
It will always take
care of you

If manifesting your goals is taking longer than you feel like it should, one of two things might be happening: either you're not doing enough to bring it into focus, or the universe is shifting and aligning to make it happen the best way it knows how. Only you know which one it really is, so check in with yourself to ensure you're doing all you can to bring what you want to you. It doesn't always happen immediately,

Friday

but it's always worth it when it arrives.

*It's easy to say "I can't." It's hard to say "I can," and it's near impossible for some
people to actually do it. Decide which person you want to be, and remember—*
the greater the risk, the greater the reward.

The more you move away from your old habits and ways of thinking, the more your brain will fight you. It's used to the old processes—that's comfortable for it. Rather than give in, have patience and be gentle while you're retraining yourself. It took you years to create those thought patterns—you're not going to undo them overnight.

Don't be embarrassed or ashamed of your fears. Everyone has them, and sharing them can help bring them into a positive light that you may not have seen otherwise.

Monday

Today, take a chance and tell someone who understands what your greatest fears are. You may get the answer you're looking for to overcome them and allow your dreams to come true.

The more you run away from the things you fear, the more they will haunt and chase you. Instead, find the courage to face them head on and stare them down. You'll be amazed when you find they weren't that bad in the first place.

Tuesday

Remember, fear is only false evidence appearing real.

Fear is something you experience when you believe you're not in control... but you're always in control. Choose your thoughts and feelings wisely, and you'll never be in despair. Doesn't that sound nice?

At some point you have to ask yourself—how much are you holding yourself back? What fears, qualms and concerns are keeping you chained in the life you used to want, versus the life you do want? Discover where you can break free and dive in with legs, arms, torso, everything.

Sometimes the freedom you seek is at your own hands.

Friday

Do you want to attract more prosperity into your life?
Who doesn't? The first step is to identify your true feelings about money and examine if that's in line with what your heart desires. If you fear it, resent it or agonize over it, it will continue to be elusive to you. Instead, change your language about it and find a point of peace. Your bank account will thank you.

Remember that when you're creating your ultimate life,

Saturday

your vision of success doesn't have to conform to societal ideals. Your success might mean living in a giant home with an ocean view, or it might mean living in a trailer in the forest. That's the beauty of this process—it's all up to you.

Notes

"*Seeing yourself as you want to be is the key to personal growth*"

Anonymous

When you think of wealth, don't just focus on the monetary values—think about wealth in a greater sense. Envelop wonderful relationships, fabulous life experiences and incredible health and well-being into the mix, and you'll find yourself becoming a more evolved, well-rounded version of yourself.

Wanting to get out of debt is an admirable goal, but it will just keep you where you are. Instead, think about becoming more prosperous. The more you think about prosperity over debt, the more prosperous you'll become—guaranteed.

If your bank account doesn't reflect what you want it to, **fake it** *until you make it! Print out a copy of your balance statement, amend the numbers the way you see fit, and post it somewhere you can see it. Then,* **feel it!** *Imagine what it will be like to have the number that you've written on that page.*

You'll never know until you try.

Finding your **inner happiness** *is key to attaining all the outer happiness you're looking for. You can have all the money, fame and toys in the world, but it doesn't mean a thing if you're not secure in yourself.*

Take time out to examine whether what you're manifesting is because you're trying to fill an emptiness or make an enhancement to your life. If it's emptiness, start to learn how to love yourself. **Everything else will follow.**

Start today with one question: "Am I loving myself today?" Are you praising yourself for good, or beating yourself up for bad? Are you enjoying the feeling of your skin, or wishing you could tear it off? Pay attention to your thoughts about yourself, and make sure you choose the good ones.

They'll carry you much further IN LIFE.

Friday

The only way to expand your capacity to receive is by expanding your capacity to give. Examine all the ways you give every day, and see if you can't give a little more. Share more of your time, insight, assistance, even wealth…then, watch your returns multiply.

Saturday

You've visualized what you want, you've paid attention to the signs, and now your dreams are coming true. Don't panic! Though it's scary when you start to realize how much control you have over your life path, freaking out will only diminish the gifts you're being given. Instead, feel gratitude. Feel proud of yourself for the work that you've done.

Then, prepare to receive more.

Sunday

Part of getting what you want is being grateful for it before it ever appears. Start today by appreciating what's coming to you. Say it out loud, write it down, whatever gets the point across. The more thankful you are for it coming into your life, the more it'll want to be in your life.

If you really want
to have your dreams come true
and your goals attained,

Monday

start by living that way right now, even if you don't have everything at your disposal just yet. The more you embrace the life you want to have, the more the life you used to have becomes a distant memory. And then before you know it, you're there.

Tuesday

When it feels like manifesting your dreams is getting exhausting, draining and time consuming, let go and have some fun. Hit the beach, watch a movie you love, have a laugh with friends, anything that can take your mind off things for a while. Then, approach your goals with a fresh attitude.

It can make all the difference.

Wednesday

Everyone wants
perfect health, and
everyone can
achieve it. When
you're feeling
under the weather,
take time out to
discover why
you feel that
way. Did you
expend too much
of yourself? Are
you *stressing*
to the point where
it makes you sick?
Are you harboring
anger and rage
that needs
to be dissipated?
When you *figure
out* the root of
your illness, you
figure out how
to *correct* it.

Your body is the product of your thoughts.

If you're unhappy with your body, it's time to examine your thought process to see what it's manifesting in you. Anxiety can bring skin problems, stress can affect weight, emotional issues can manifest in stomach trouble. Today, look at any health issues that plague you and see how they correspond with your lifestyle and train of thought. It will help you identify the problem, and ultimately, fix it.

Friday

Do you know your worth? *If you don't know your worth, how can the universe know your worth? Writing down just a few things that make you worthy every morning before you start your day solidifies the reasons you should get everything you want in life, and more. Start examining what makes you worthy today.*

When you think about love, what is it that you see and feel?
Does it bring about feelings of joy and warmth,
or does it make you feel hurt and sad?

To create the love that you want, you need to get to the root of your feelings and ensure your mind and heart are in tune. Without that unity, you're fated to repeat past mistakes.

Before you start trying to manifest a relationship, start by understanding the relationship you have with yourself. If you don't feel attractive, likeable or worthy of love, guess what?

That's the kind of person you're going to attract to you, if you attract anyone at all. How can anyone learn to love you if you don't set the example? Find little ways to love yourself every day.

Sunday

Monday

Looking to someone else to create your *happiness* for you will guarantee that you will be disappointed, because nobody can create your happiness quite like you can. If you're looking to someone else to make your dreams come true and you're feeling disappointed, shift your focus and regroup, set your own goals, and reset your intention. It's the only way to *achieve* what you *want* out of life.

Tuesday

Don't look for your relationship to give you what you feel you don't have—look to yourself to do it. Only you have the strength and the power to fill those voids that you feel inside. If your life is less than stellar, take a look at what you're expecting others to do for you rather than doing it for yourself.

It all starts and ends WITH YOU.

Wednesday

Instead of trying to fix your job, fix your relationship or fix your outside world,
try looking within to find something to fix. What we lack in the real world is
actually what we lack in the spiritual world, and that can always be found within.

When you start with you, *everything else follows.*

There are days where you feel strong and positive, and there are days where you feel weak and negative. On the days you feel strong, concentrate your good feelings on someone else you know in your life that could use a pick-me-up. That way, when you need one, it'll come to you.

Instead of asking what the universe can do for you, why not ask what you can do for the universe? Take a look around you and note what little things might pop up asking for your assistance, like trash on the ground that needs to be thrown out or an older woman needing help with her groceries.

Friday

When you help others, help comes to you.

You can't expect the universe to behave a certain way unless you're behaving in that certain way. Periodically taking the time out to decide what message you're sending to the world will help you stay on track in achieving your goals, or get back on it if you've lost your way.

Saturday

If you believe that the world is against you, nothing good is coming your way and you'll never get your heart's desire, then you're right. "In order to succeed, your desire for success should be greater than your fear of failure."
—Bill Cosby

Sometimes, the key to getting what you want is detaching yourself from it. If you're obsessively hanging on to thoughts of riches, cars and that seemingly unattainable love, let go and connect to yourself instead. Once you do, you'll find you have more power to bring it to you.

Monday

Know that even when it feels the most hopeless, the universe is conspiring to bring you everything you deserve because it wants to see you happy and successful. So instead of cursing it, praise it. It's not always easy—especially in the tough times—but believing the universe will bring you what you desire will **make it happen faster than you realize.**

Whether something in your life is a blessing or a curse is up to you. Today, take a look at the things you see as curses and try to look at them from an alternate position. Try to find the good in everything. That way, everything good can find you.

Just because you're looking for what you think you don't have doesn't mean you don't have it. In fact, often times it's right under your very nose. Taking notice of what you have, rather than what you don't, reacquaints you with the end result you're looking for.

Thursday

Make time to appreciate what you have today, and watch yourself prosper as a result.

When you focus on the positive, the solution is already there—
and that applies to any situation. The next time you find yourself faced
with trouble, find the bright side and focus on it.

Friday

It'll make things that much easier to deal with,
and you'll solve the issue that much quicker.

We always fear falling back into old habits means we're suffering a setback, but it's only a setback if you fall and stay fallen. When you feel yourself resorting to old thought patterns and behaviors, stop. Take a breath. Analyze why it is you're reverting, then let go and move forward.

Saturday

Only you have the power to keep choosing to move forward.

The fastest way to ensure that you won't achieve everything you desire is to shroud your wishes in darkness and doubt. Make sure you're finding new ways each day to believe in yourself and what you desire. Believing in your dreams and being devoted to their realization will ensure they come true.

Monday

Remember that the closer you get to getting what you desire, the more likely it is that you'll start to self-destruct. That's because old thought patterns are threatening the new ones coming in. When you feel an internal struggle, rise above it and take control.

Good things happen when you do.

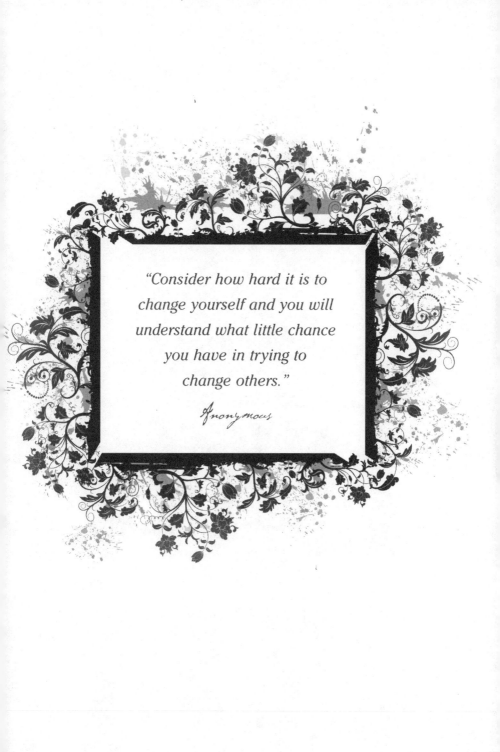

"Consider how hard it is to change yourself and you will understand what little chance you have in trying to change others."

Anonymous

Don't be in a rush to get to where you're going to be.

Tuesday

Instead, settle back and enjoy the ride—that's part of the fun, and it'll ensure that you get what's coming to you when you take some time to enjoy the process rather than endure it.

Have you noticed some unpredictable events coming into your life, usually at random, seemingly without meaning? That's the universe's way of letting you know it's at work, helping you manifest your heart's desires. Pay attention to the bizarre things that cross your path today, and regard them with a knowing smile. It's all part of the plan.

Being *surrounded* by lots of negativity usually comes from within—like always attracts like. When you notice yourself enveloped in negative drama, take a moment to look at the inner workings of your brain to deconstruct where you're holding negative thoughts, and why. Then, *release* them and *move forward*.
You must always be moving forward.

Feeling hatred for someone or something never feels good, so why not replace your feelings of hatred with love? Instead of being mad about traffic, embrace the time with yourself, and enjoy singing along with the music. When your significant other does something to make you mad, focus on what makes you happy about them instead.

Love is thousands of times more powerful than hate.

Practicing *finding the good in everything takes time, but it's worth it.*
When you're tempted to look for the bad in people, places and things,
replace those thoughts with good ones and say them out loud, just for good measure.

It will **remind** *the universe of what you want in life, rather than what you don't.*

Saturday

N. Y.

Patterns repeat in your life when you're not learning the lesson you're supposed to learn. When you find yourself saying, "I've been here before," it's time to look at what you're refusing to look at. That's the only way you'll change your behavior, and start moving toward your goals.

Monday

Remember that all the bad things you weather, all the challenges you face, all the seemingly insurmountable things are all just practice to prepare you for the really, really good stuff. Look at all the tough times you've been through and marvel at how you've survived, and the good that's come from those moments. You might be surprised at what you find.

Tuesday

When you think small, you achieve small. When you think big, guess what?
Don't let negativity or your ego hold you back from dreaming up the best life possible.
Dream large, dream vibrantly, then embrace it and prepare. It's always coming to you.

Wednesday

You can only share what you have, and you can only have what you share. So if you wish for the universe to be generous with you, be generous with it. Give yourself in every way without depleting yourself. Do so selflessly for others, but also for selfish joy. Then, sit back and watch what happens.

How do you know you're
on the right path to
reaching your life's goals?

Thursday

It depends on how you feel. When you feel happy and alive, you know you're on track. When you feel down in the dumps, you've lost your way. Take a look at how you feel throughout your day, then make a choice. It's all up to you.

Friday

It's always a good idea to take a break from the rigors of life, but the one thing you should
never break from is dreaming of and visualizing your life goals. When you find yourself
feeling as though your desires are work, try taking a break from something else and refocus.

Never lose sight of what you want.

Saturday

Each day you have a **choice**— *you can live in the "what ifs," the "maybes" and the "hows," or you can experience every moment as it happens, living fully and freely in the now. Guess which one brings you* **closer** *to your dreams? Today, disregard the hows and whys, and just focus on the wonder of now.*

When you feel yourself lacking in a certain area, don't rear back in an attempt to preserve what you have—instead, give and see what it brings up for you. Show someone love, help people you know with something they need assistance with, share half of your last dollar with someone in need. Then, revel in the good feeling that comes from that.

It will only bring you more.

Monday

It's easy to find a way to con ourselves into thinking we're doing enough to *manifest our dreams* into reality, but there's always something more that can be done. Are you exploring every avenue? Watching for the signs? Taking all the necessary steps? Today, *challenge* yourself to go further, and see *where it takes* you.

Tuesday

You know the saying—it's always darkest before the dawn.
When it seems like all the decks are stacked against you,
it's only because you're being tested.

Do you really want what's coming to you, or are you going to back down just before
it gets there? When you feel like quitting, it's just a sign that you're almost there.

Fight the urge.

It's hard to remember that life's toughest lessons often yield the greatest rewards, especially when you're going through them.

Reflecting on your toughest times and seeing the bright side helps to get you through when you think all is lost. Looking for the up in every down is just one more way to encourage positivity in your life.

Wednesday

Thursday

Do you feel like you're stuck in the same place?

Sometimes we're in a holding pattern while the universe figures out the best course of action, but other times we're finding ways to hold ourselves back from achieving our goals. Only you know if you're self-sabotaging, so take a good, hard look in the mirror and figure out how much of your position is because of you.

Friday

Remember that although the universe wants you to have everything you want when you want it, some things take longer than others—and a lot of that has to do with how prepared you are to accept your gifts. Don't forget to look within to determine whether or not you really deem yourself worthy of getting what you want. That's part of the puzzle.

It's time to take stock. How many of your desires have come true, and how many still remain unrequited? Figure out which dreams work for you and which ones don't, then refocus on what you want today. Remember, there's no limitation on what you want—you can refine and change your mind whenever you wish.

One of the keys to giving and receiving is love, but you can't give of yourself if you don't love yourself. Make a list of all the things you love about yourself, and revel in the good feelings it brings up. Then, share those loving feelings with people around you. Watch your happiness surge, and the good things will start rolling into your life!

Know that you can have it all,

and the only thing that limits you from having it all is you. Dream large,
no matter how strange or unreal it may seem. It will make you feel good, and
you never know what might happen….

It's tempting to sink into doubt and depression because it's a learned behavior—it's something you're used to. Don't dishonor those feelings, but don't dwell in them either—that will just set you further away from your goal.

Tuesday

Happy thoughts bring happy results!

When you're thinking about the future, the Law of Attraction is working. When you're thinking of the past, the Law of Attraction is working. Remember, no matter what you're thinking about, the Law of Attraction is working. So wouldn't you want to make sure you think good thoughts? Become aware of your thought process, and choose the good ones.

The definition of insanity is approaching the same situation with the same reaction and expecting different results. Instead of doing the same old thing in the same old situation, challenge yourself by trying something new. Who knows what good might come of it until you try?

Thursday

Feeling money strain is no fun, but the more you focus on it, the more you feel it. Play some fun money games instead, like writing yourself a check for the amount you'd like to see in your bank account, use white-out and alter the statement on your balance, or go to the store and imagine all the things you could buy with all the money in your wallet.

Your prosperity will be overflowing in no time!

It's easy to love the big things in life, but do you take pleasure in the little things? Not all of life's joys need to be ginormous, monumental events. Sometimes they're as simple as a good cup of coffee, a half day at work or praise from a loved one. Take note and make a list of all the small blessings in your life. It'll lead to bigger ones down the road.

If you're hanging on to old pain, you're blocking yourself from seeing, feeling and experiencing all the good that you desire. Find constructive ways to let it out, whether that means screaming into a pillow or writing your frustrations in a diary.

Sunday

Moving the negativity out of you makes more room for positivity.

Complaining is the world's favorite pastime, but you can rise above it and change your life in the process. Think of how much energy you expend in complaining about things, and flip it.

Monday

Every time you find the need to complain, stop yourself and find a reason to be thankful, or talk about something you love. Your psyche will thank you.

Every day gives you the gift of a lesson, so what's your lesson today? Look at the past week and see if you can find the lessons that you've learned, and how you've improved your life day by day based on what you've learned.

Nobody else can create your life like the way you can.
When you find yourself looking to someone else to help you make
your story happen when it's something you could do on your own, stop and examine
what it is inside you that needs to feel whole, then fix it yourself.
Other people can help you on your path, but they cannot walk it for you.

Do you want to feel free? Freedom is a choice, so why not choose it?
Break free of the shackles you've put upon yourself and dare to live wildly and happily. For some it may mean scaling a mountain, for others it might mean ordering something different for lunch. Whatever it might be, test your boundaries and see how amazing it makes you feel!

"I've come to believe that each of us has a personal calling that's as unique as a fingerprint—and that the best way to succeed is to discover what you love and then find a way to offer it to others in the form of service, working hard, and also allowing the energy of the universe to lead you."

Oprah Winfrey

Your head is full of wiring and thoughts and things floating around, and sometimes it gets going so fast that it's hard to slow it down. Using meditation helps to calm the mind and refocus it on your goals, especially when you hold your desire at the forefront of your brain and think about it and it alone.

Friday

Take some time out to focus your thoughts on one of your goals. Just make sure you're prepared when it comes to you quicker than you thought!

Saturday

Not every answer that comes to you is the right answer—it's up to you to determine what works and what doesn't. As the universe works at bringing you your heart's desires, it doesn't always find the perfect way to do it. But don't become frustrated. Instead, express gratitude for the solution you've been presented with, and ask for a more appropriate one. The universe will respond in kind.

Just because you've attained one goal doesn't mean you can't attain another. In fact, you should be challenging the universe just as much as it challenges you! Every time you see one of your goals come true, create a new one—and delight in the process of doing so!

Even the tiniest of thoughts, the most insignificant of dreams,
are tied to something bigger and brighter for you. So pay attention
to those thoughts that you have in your sleep and remember when
you wake up...see if you can find the *deeper meaning* in them.

It might tell you more about what you want than even you know.

Those who don't actively dream their life are doomed to experience chaos, heartache and trouble, while those who do actively dream their life are destined to experience joy, prosperity and wild abundance.

N. Y.

Which one do you choose? *Start by planning an hour, then a day, and maybe a whole week, then see how close it was to what you envisioned.*

DO YOU JUST
PRETEND?

Do you talk the talk and walk the walk, or do you just pretend? The difference between the two is one helps you get what you want, the other keeps you in wanting. Pay attention to how you speak about your life, how you carry yourself and how you treat others. It's the window to the inner workings of your soul.

Thursday

Approaching life with a mundane attitude and expecting miracles is like strapping on skis to take a walk down the street—not only does it not work, it doesn't make sense. Find your zest in life. Live with unbridled joy. It's the only way to encourage everything you want to come to you.

Friday

The more you try to manipulate, force, cajole and position your life, the less likely it is that you're going to get the results you want. Trying to control your life on an active level doesn't do you justice, which is why visioning is so useful—it gently nudges the universe in the right direction without forcing it. Make sure you're being gentle when you ask for your wish, and not demanding.

It's a subtle difference, but it makes all the difference in the world.

Identifying what no longer serves you and making space for something new is helpful both literally and physically. Got a pile of clothing you never wear anymore? Donate it to charity. Hanging on to memories that only make you sad? Find a way to release them and let them go. It'll help make room for more good things to come your way.

your mind, but you don't have to accept them. Just change your min
of the exact opposite. With practice, your mind will start doing th
's possible it 's just a matter of choice. Negative thoughts will com
mind, but you don't have to accept them. Just change your mind a
the exact opposite. With practice, your mind will start doing that
's possible it 's just a matter of choice. Negative thoughts will

If you're thinking
"it's too late,"

Sunday

then you're probably right. But if you're thinking, "It's never too late," you're right about that too. Today, discover what it's never too late for, be it an "I'm sorry" or a change in your course of action or a snack after dinner. You never know what you can allow yourself to have until you just allow yourself to have it.

Monday

*Do you blame yourself, beat yourself up and generally make yourself feel bad
for things that you do? Stop. Every time you feel the need to be hard on yourself, respond
with love instead and revel in the feelings of good that surround you.*

Remember, you're the marker by which everyone learns how to treat you.

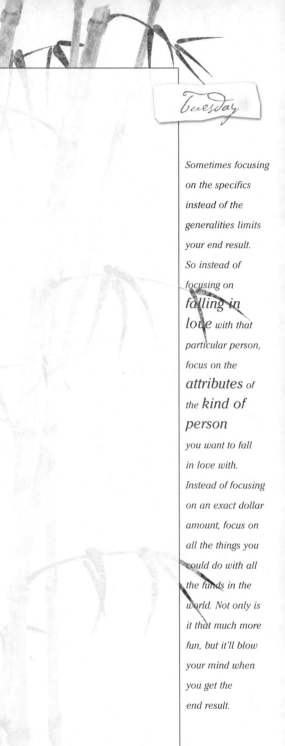

Sometimes focusing on the specifics instead of the generalities limits your end result. So instead of focusing on *falling in love* with that particular person, focus on the *attributes* of the *kind of person* you want to fall in love with. Instead of focusing on an exact dollar amount, focus on all the things you could do with all the funds in the world. Not only is it that much more fun, but it'll blow your mind when you get the end result.

What you resist persists, so take a moment to determine what it is you're resisting today. When you face up to it, the blocks will be removed, and

you'll be right back on track.

Thursday

If **getting** what you wanted were super *easy*, you **wouldn't appreciate** it as much. So when you're having one of those days where you wish everything would just drop in your lap, think of life as a piñata. Sometimes it takes a few attempts, but the **more you try**, the better chance you have at getting to the sweet stuff inside.

When *good things* happen for you, do you ever get the feeling that they're fleeting and they're not going to last? That's the quickest way to ensure they're going to *disappear*.

Instead, revel in the *good feeling* that comes along with good things happening, and watch those good things *multiply*.

Remember that there are as many hours in the day as you want or need there to be to get things done. If there's not, what are you wasting your time on?

Find ways that you can maximize your hours in an effort to bring your goals closer to you, even if it means cutting down on your TV time. It's worth it.

Saturday

Sunday

Sometimes the universe presents you with two options in solving a dilemma,
which can be quite perplexing. Which one do you choose?
What if you choose wrong? But you can never choose wrong because
the universe will realign to fit your decision. Have confidence
in your choices and everything else will fall into place.

Worrying is just a symptom of a bigger cause. When you feel yourself spinning into a spiral of doubt, stop and close your eyes, then dig to the root of what's really bothering you. It'll make your problem that much easier to deal with, and get you back on the right path to achieving your dreams.

Tuesday

It can get exhausting doing all that wishing, dreaming, visualizing, sign-watching, step-taking and all the other things you need to do to bring the life you want into existence.

So take a break!

Even as you're recharging your batteries, the universe is still working away at your goals.

Wednesday

Do you hear that little voice in your head that says you're not worth it, you don't deserve
it, it will never come to you? That's not the universe talking, that's your monkey mind.
Instead of paying attention, ignore it. Occupy it with something. Do what you have to do
to get it out of the way so you can go back to thinking happy thoughts.

Thursday

or are you living it as perfectly as you can right this very second? Take a moment to examine how you're approaching your life on a daily basis, and see if you can't change your own mind about what perfection is. When you do, it all falls into place.

All challenges come with dreams, all dreams come with challenges. The sooner you understand that, the easier it is to face up to the road blocks that life seems to throw in your way. Take a look at a recent challenge and see if you can figure out the dream behind it.

Friday

It's all a part of putting the bigger puzzle together.

When you feel incomplete and unhappy, it's hard for the fun, happy, good things to come to you. Take a moment to figure out how you can complete yourself or make yourself happier without looking for some- one else to do it for you. It will feel that much more fulfilling, and solidify your path to abundance.

Part of receiving amazingly stupendous things in your life is knowing you deserve to...but do you know you deserve to, or do you pretend like you do? Today is the day to address why you pretend you deserve to, and how you can change that into knowing. You'll be amazed at how things change when you change that simple thing.

Sunday

When it feels like your goals are far out of reach,
take some time out to tell yourself how it's all going to go down. Say it out loud, don't feel silly!
Just explain where you are, what's going on and how it's all going to be so amazing, then revel
in the feeling of fabulousness you get when your story reaches its ultimate goal. That's how
you're going to feel when it happens to you.

The more you live in the past, the less chance you have of catching up to the future. Are you thinking about yesterday more than today or tomorrow? Shift your thoughts to the present and future, and revel in the joy that brings you. Remember, you can't move forward if you're always looking backwards.

Knowing how your dreams are going to come true isn't important, but knowing your dreams is. When you worry yourself with the hows, it keeps you from experiencing the end result. Focus on letting go of the process and enjoy the journey instead.

Wednesday

*Life becomes challenging because the universe is shifting and changing
ever closer to helping us in achieving our goals—even in the most difficult times.
Instead of fighting it, ride the wave and rest assured that it's all moving toward
a greater end. The more you fight it, the harder it gets.*

Are things starting to feel complacent? Move! Whether it be walking, jumping, dancing or just flinging your arms about, whipping up the energy around you can give that little shift you need for things to fall into place.

Friday

Saturday

There are days where it seems like everyone is bringing you down, and days where it feels like everyone is lifting you up. The one constant in those to experiences is you. Figure out what you're doing to encourage both events, then hang on to the good stuff and **discard the bad.**

Notes

*Spend ten minutes listening
to the birds today.
Be grateful for their song.*

Sunday

*Part of asking, believing and receiving is taking responsibility for every step of the process.
You can't just ask and expect it will happen—you have to follow through.
Take a look at how much follow through you're giving, asking, believing and receiving.*

Is there something more you could be doing?

The perfect antidote to doubt is analyzing what you're doubting and why—but you really need to get to the root of the doubt to fix it. Are you doubting because you don't think you deserve it? Figure out why you think you don't. Are you doubting because the goal isn't in line with who you are?

Monday

Choose a goal that's better. That's how you get what you want.

Tuesday

To experience the good, you also have to embrace the bad. When you feel tempted to run in the other direction at the sight of strife, run toward it instead and jump into it head on. Things won't seem as bad if you do.

Take a moment to *step forward* in time and look back on the last week of your life. Now imagine that everything went exactly according to plan. Your job was stress free and you got a raise, romance came your way, good fortune met you at every turn.

Now revel in that *feeling — take it all in and expand it*. When you open your eyes, it'll be real because you felt it and made it so.

Believing in limits only serves to limit yourself, and who wants that? Look at the limits you place on yourself, be they small or *large*, and discover how you can break through them to live a happier, healthier, more abundant life.

You might be surprised.

N. Y.

M

There is a subtle difference between good pushing and bad pushing when it comes
to manifesting your dreams. **Good pushing** *is met with successive movement*
forward, bad pushing *is met with* **resistance and walls**.
Figure out which one you're doing and realign accordingly.

Saturday

There's one instance where looking to the past is beneficial, and that's if you're learning from it. Take a moment to look at the things you can do differently today than you did yesterday, and enjoy the positive changes and movement you're making. It's all about taking those steps in the right direction.

Your life is like a Choose Your Own Adventure book, except you create the choices and the adventures all on your own. What kind of adventures do you want to have? Write them down, study them and bring them into your consciousness. Then, prepare for something even better than you imagined. The universe loves surprises!

Monday

Your dreams can tell you more about your subconscious thoughts
than you realize. When you remember them, write them down. Were they scary or pleasant?
Were there signs that repeated? Paying attention to your dreams can be the key that helps
unlock the door you feel like you can't get through.

Tuesday

Realize that when you try to control something outside of you—be it people, events, or how your goals come to you—all you're doing is putting restrictions on the freewheeling nature of the universe, which only serves to impede your progress. Just let go! Things will come to you faster if you do.

Conflict is inevitable.

Wednesday

Without friction, there's no life. But what can change the conflict for you is how you choose to look at it. What can you learn from it? Is this something you need to keep in your life, or should you extract it? Only you know for sure what will help keep you on your path, so ask questions and act according to what makes you happy.

Anger can act as a virus. It's infectious.

Have you ever been in a situation where an argument starts and the more heated the other person gets, the more heated you get? You have the power to diffuse the situation and turn things around. Disconnect from the emotions of the situation and take a step back. Don't absorb what the other person says. The more ways you can keep yourself feeling good, the better.

Friday

The next time
you feel
compelled
to talk about
someone else,
stop and
think. Is
talking about
them helping to
achieve a greater
good, or is it
only serving
to be mean
and spiteful?
Remember that
positive
actions
bring
positive
things. That
might change
your mind about
what you want
to say.

Need an instant pick-me-up
to help those happy vibes come into your life?

Get started by doing a little dance. Seriously! Jump up and wave your hands in the air. Get a little groove going. You'll feel silly, you'll laugh at yourself...and that's the point. Anything to get you smiling will help that positive energy come your way.

Sunday

Your home says more about your mental state than you think. If you're perpetually single and wish you were in a relationship, look around you. Do you have pictures of people alone on your walls and fridge, or are there symbols of togetherness and partnership? Making some simple changes in your décor can help **shift your intention** *in the* **right direction.**

Monday

If writing out your desires doesn't work for you, find some other way to express your desires. Maybe you can paint them, draw them, sculpt them…any kind of creative process that brings you into that mode of thinking and feeling what you ultimately want can help strengthen the vibration of bringing it to you.

I. I doesn't have to be perfect it just has to be.

pure.

Anger is a habit, and it's a habit we can all break. The next time you feel yourself getting hot under the collar, take a moment to step outside yourself and analyze what you're getting mad at and why...

and also how it makes you feel. Remember, anger just stops the flow of abundance. The more you're aware of that, the more you want to choose happy feelings.

Tuesday

Wednesday

If you're having negative thoughts about something, **don't worry**—*positive thoughts are much more powerful than negative ones. However, negative thoughts are our system's warning feature. Do some* **deep** *meditation to figure out what's bothering you beneath the surface. It'll help make you* **feel better** *on every level.*

Negativity can be ADDICTIVE,

infectious and hard to fight against—it prevails throughout so much in our society. The next time you feel yourself getting sucked in, stop. Take a moment to breathe. Decide that you don't want to be a part of it, but you understand and respect that some people do. Then, watch how much more wonder rains into your life!

Friday

They say that what you dislike in others is only what you dislike in yourself.
The next time you find yourself complaining about someone you know or passing judgment
on someone you don't, stop and think about what you're saying and how it applies to you.
Not only will this help you reach a higher plane, it keeps the positive juices flowing,

which can only lead to more abundance!

Saturday

It can be hard to have confidence when you have darkness in your past, but living in your past is a surefire way to ensure the future isn't any better. Instead, make a note every day about something you like about yourself, and watch that list grow. Soon the past will be a distant memory and you'll feel like a million bucks! Remember, like attracts like....

Remember that nobody is above you, and nobody is beneath you—we are all equal at our core. The minute you feel tempted to put yourself above someone else, your ego is in control, trying to make you superior. Ask yourself why. The same thing goes if you're trying to put someone above you—why do you see yourself as being unworthy of their equality? The devil is always in the details, and only you know the details.

Instead of asking how people can be of service to you, try asking how you can be of service to them. It's great to receive and to give, so make sure you're giving and getting to keep the flow of abundance coming your way.

Tuesday

When someone you
know achieves some-
thing grand, do you find
yourself feeling happy
for them, or jealous of
them? If it's the latter,
ask yourself why your
friend doesn't deserve
to have good things too
and address the envy
within you. It's the
surest way to transform
it into happiness

Saying "I can't" will only ensure you can't…and the more you say it, the more true it becomes. Try saying you can…or better yet, why not just do? You'll be amazed at what is possible when you remove the mental blocks holding you back.

Wednesday

Are you who you are, or are you what you have? When everything is stripped away, are you still someone you want to be around? If the answer is no, it's time to evolve into someone you adore. You're not going to be able to change the world around you

unless you start with you.

When you start to realize how much of your life's happenings are really up to you, it can become tempting to beat yourself up, asking, "Why did I do those things in the past?" Stop. For one, living in the past keeps you from moving forward. For two, beating yourself up just enforces negativity, which defeats the whole process. Instead, congratulate yourself on having figured it all out, and decide what you want to manifest next!

Sometimes, it's just a matter of deciding what you want to be an expression of.
Do you want to be an expression of happiness, health and wonderment?

Saturday

Or do you want to be an expression of despair, desolation and abandonment? Be mindful of which expression you choose, from the moment you awake to the moment you return to sleep.

Does it feel like your goals just aren't coming true? It may be time to ask yourself if you've set your sights too high, too soon. Certainly the universe wants to give you what you want, but it can't if you don't believe in it. Try scaling back a little bit to something more believable for you, then think loftier when you achieve it.

Sunday

Sometimes all it can take to turn your world around is a smile. So simple, so basic, yet so effective! Try sharing a smile with a stranger on the street, or just give yourself one in the mirror—especially on days when you feel your lowest. It can help turn things around for you!

Monday

When you get what you want, the trick to keeping it is to continue to hold it in your consciousness. Don't just abandon your dream because it's been achieved—revel in it! Enjoy it! Thank your lucky stars that it's a part of your life every day! Not only will that ensure your gift remains, but it will also encourage more to come to you.

Notes

Nourish your inner garden. Cherish five things that bring you joy, peace and love. Through this practice, you will learn to understand yourself and be aware of your path.

Wednesday

If you're finding it too hard to have faith in yourself to manifest your dreams, *try finding something else to have faith in—the tree in your front yard, a rock you picked up on a hike, the barista you order your coffee from every morning. Not only does it take some of the pressure off you, it keeps you on track even when you think you're off.*

Hoarding things all to yourself is the surest way to lose them. Instead, why not share in your good fortune and help others get a little joy with which to accomplish their dreams? How you choose to share is up to you, just remember—what goes around comes around.

Thursday

Wouldn't you rather it be good than bad?

Friday

It's never easy to see someone else in despair, but trying to help them when they're not ready to receive help or attempting to force them in a direction they're not ready to go in will only cause both of you strife. Instead, give them the room and gentle support they need to find their own way. They will come to you when they're ready, and you'll have more energy to help them.

The more you try to attach yourself to something, the more it will want to leave—doing this is just another matter of trying to exhibit control over something you feel you have no control over. When you feel the urge to cling, turn within and determine what's going on in your mind instead. Letting go and letting things flow the way they need and want to will bring you much greater rewards in the end.

If you look at the world and see chaos and destruction, it's time to filter out what you're reading and watching. Being aware of your surroundings is one thing, becoming engulfed in them is entirely another. Try to find balance in your media diet to ensure your positive, creative process isn't being subconsciously blocked.

When we are praying, wishing, dreaming, hoping, imagining and desiring, we tend to look up as if to send our thoughts to the heavens. When we are sad, lonely, blue, despondent, heartbroken and depressed, we look down.

Today, pay attention to where you're looking—both literally and figuratively— and watch your perspective **change.**

Being abundant in all senses of the word isn't just about manifesting and being grateful, it's also about being aware. Sometimes the abundance creeps in so simply and subtly that we don't even notice we've started living a completely different life. Today, take notice of where you are and embrace it.

And enjoy it!

The thing you have to remember is you've always had it all—it's just been laying dormant inside you. Today, find new ways to electrify that desire and drum up new goals, places to see and things to do that make you infinitely happy. It's always a process, but it's a good one!

Thursday

It can be hard to see the silver lining on the cloud when you're in the middle of it, but even the toughest of life's moments don't last forever. When you're in the middle of a dark spot, take some time out to nurture yourself and remind yourself that this too shall pass. Darkness is just a sign of growth, and giving up just ensures you won't reap the rewards!

Friday

Anything and everything can become a symbol for us to guide our lives by—it's up to you to choose which ones mean something to you. Does a certain street sign bring thoughts of something that happened on a good day? Does passing it mean today is going to be good? Little symbols like this can help you create your day into something fabulous—don't miss the opportunity to use tools in your manifestations.

Do you look at life as being for you or against you?

Is waking up in the morning a chore, or is it a ritualistic occasion you derive pleasure from? Even in your darkest hour, choosing to look at the flow of life as being in your favor only helps solidify it into reality, changing your perspective for the better. Pay attention to how you look at your own life today, tomorrow, and every day.

There is nothing wrong with asking for or expecting miracles—
you're entitled to them! And how will the universe know that you want one unless you tell it? Take a moment today to figure out what kind of miracle you want in your life, then address it in a way that the universe will understand it as a request above all the other manifestations you have. This special attention will not only provide it faster, but in a more special way than all the rest!

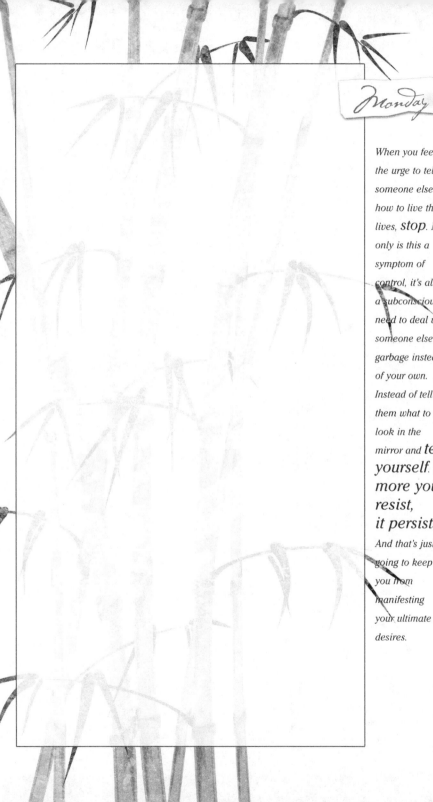

Monday

*When you feel the urge to tell someone else how to live their lives, **stop**. Not only is this a symptom of control, it's also a subconscious need to deal with someone else's garbage instead of your own. Instead of telling them what to do, look in the mirror and **tell yourself**. The **more you resist, it persists**. And that's just going to keep you from manifesting your ultimate desires.*

Are you aware of the wonderment that colors your life,

or do you wander through unobservant and unimpressed? Try taking notice of every little thing, good and bad...and if it's bad, try finding the good in it. Before you know it, you won't have to work very hard at this at all, and the creative flow will be working through you like never before!

Wednesday

Throughout all of this manifesting, all of this creation and all of this work, it becomes easy to lose sight of one's self. Don't forget to celebrate you—without you, none of this would be possible! Take time out to enjoy yourself—relax, have some fun, treat yourself to something good. **It all starts and ends with you.**

Do you live fully and express yourself openly and honestly in everything you do, or do you cage yourself, bind yourself and hold yourself back from being the real you? Today, examine the various kinds of limitations you put on yourself, and figure out how to break yourself free.

Liberation is an incredible feeling.

Challenges will come in all forms, no matter what you do to try to avoid them— especially if you try to avoid them! Determine what it is you fear in the challenges you face, and face that first.

Starting with the root of the fear will make the actual challenge that much easier to flow through.

Friday

Saturday

When it comes to **manifesting** *your desires, your mind is like a fertile playground just waiting to be watered. Spend some time really playing with the recesses of your mind, both as an* active and passive *participant. Watch what it brings up, and see where you can guide it. The two of you can* work together *to make your dreams true!*

HOW FAR CAN YOU GO?

How high can you soar? How much can you achieve? Only you know the answer, so ask yourself the question and see what you come up with. Sometimes, that's all the universe needs to bring it to you.

Monday

Infinite abundance isn't just a gift, it's a responsibility. Today, ensure that
you're being responsible with your gift so that abundance can continue to flow to you.

It's all about keeping the cycle going.

Tuesday

Remember that a mental avenue must be provided for the Law of Abundance to work through…and that means ensuring your thought process is moving in that direction, unobstructed, undeterred. Find the little mental blocks that are plaguing you today, and knock them down. It's time to open the floodgates!

Wednesday

It's about surrendering with glee, opening yourself up to all the possibilities and choosing the ones that flow to you with the most beneficial path attached to them. Make sure your surrender isn't apathetic, but instead, joyous and co-conspiratorial!

Every step you choose to take in your life path is a graduation of the moment before it, every realized dream a step up from where you were before. Instead of seeing manifestation as work, see it as evolution, steps forward in time, all moving you toward a greater good.

Thursday

The Law of Attraction will thank you.

The more you hang on to unharmonious experiences with people, places or things, the less you allow yourself to feel the goodness, abundance, health and happiness. Instead of dwelling, replay the experience in your mind and give it the outcome you wish it could have had. Then, move forward, ever gracefully, ever happily.

If you're hard on yourself, you sometimes don't realize how hard you are on other people, too. Today, learn to have compassion for not only those you push, but also for you. Living gently and peacefully only allows for more fabulousness to come your way.

Saturday

Living with intention is like planting seeds—

*you start with an idea, you think it through, you use the universe to water it
and you watch it grow. See what seeds of intention you can plant and grow today,
and how they help transform your life for weeks and months to follow.*

*Do you learn by seeing or doing? One isn't better than the other, but try the opposite
for a day and see how it changes your perspective, what feelings it brings up,
and how you address it. You never know what opportunities can arise from changing your routine.*

If you find your surroundings to be counterproductive to
manifesting your goals and dreams, change your surroundings.

Tuesday

That may mean a general tidying and a fresh coat of paint, or taking your
manifesting meditations to a hilltop or oceanside, or maybe as drastic as finding
a new home! Only you know what's best for you. Go to it!

You've given thanks for your abundance, the continual flow of it, the universe…but have you thanked yourself for acting as the vessel to help provide the catalyst for it? Don't forget to appreciate the most key unit to this whole experience of manifestation—you!

Wednesday

Creation comes from love. Today, address all the things you love in and about your life, and where appropriate, speak it out loud! It feels good to share love, and feeling good is what manifesting is all about!

When you work on manifesting your dreams, do you ask timidly, or does your mental voice boom with confidence and bravado? Watch yourself when you're asking for what you want, and see what kind of language and tenor your brain uses when it's conjuring up dreams.

Make sure you're asking with gusto and confidence!

Notes

Saturday

What you focus on expands, so make sure what you're focusing on is what you want to expand. Today, look at the molehills you're making into mountains and **determine how they serve you...and eliminate them if they don't.**

As a child, you used your imagination to become a firefighter, a detective, nearly anything you wanted to be. Somewhere along the way you learned not to. Try using that childlike nature to imagine your future today. Get lost in the experience!

Sunday

Not only is it fun, it's effective.

You don't have to fight your feelings every step of the way, but if you find a thought repeating itself, it might be that you're not honoring it and letting it go. Instead of trying to push a repetitive thought away, close your eyes and allow yourself to feel it fully. Then, if it doesn't serve you, let it go so you can make way for newer, better, more abundant thoughts.

Don't worry about how you're going to deal with attaining everything you want—it just puts undue stress on yourself, and who needs more stress? Find the inner strength you need to trust in the unknown, and watch things unfold.

Wednesday

Have you created your vision board yet? Do you have someplace where you can gaze upon the things you most desire to help *you* visualize *and* attain *what you want? Remember that your vision board isn't static—when you achieve something, add something new in its place.*

It'll keep the prosperity coming!

N. Y.

When you live your life lovingly, fully and happily, good things **naturally** *come your way. When you live your life angrily and stressfully, good things* **fall away** *because it's not in tune with your nature. Today, take a moment to connect with yourself and figure out what's really going on inside of you. It's a great way to match up your insides with your outsides.*

*One of the keys to manifesting all your dreams is to discover, enjoy and envelop
yourself in patience. The more impatient you are, the more you push away your end result.
Try to find a way to enjoy the process—the reward will be that much sweeter.*

Saturday

The important thing to remember is when you feel yourself sliding into old habits and beliefs, make sure you have the presence of mind to pull yourself out again before you get in too deep. It will save you from having to retrace too many of your steps in the future.

Sunday

Letting go of your fear of losing something takes just one step:
realizing that the things you fear losing can always be recreated somewhere, some day, somehow, as long as you believe, and as long as you're actively involved in your life's creation. Take a look at what you fear losing today and see if you can't dissolve that fear with this simple solution.

Monday

Remember that you are the barometer by which everyone else learns how to treat you, so it's best if you treat yourself with love, kindness and respect. Find new ways to love yourself today, not just to watch your life's path unfold the way you want it to, but also to give yourself a much-needed energy boost!

It's never easy
to forgive someone
who has hurt you.

Tuesday

either on purpose or by accident. But taking the time out to accept someone's apology clears you of the burden of carrying around angst and anger that festers and rots inside you. The more you let go of the badness, the more goodness can come in!

Wednesday

Have you noticed lately that everything is turning up roses? If not, it's about time you did.
Make a list as you go through your day of all the things that are good in your life.

Focusing on the positive only brings more to you.

Thursday

Having **peace of mind** isn't so much about ignoring or running away from issues as it is about **having strength**. When you feel yourself devolving into old patterns, **flex** your mental muscle and pull yourself out of it. Only you have the power.

It's tempting to have expectations of exactly how everything is going to turn out, and feeling disappointment when it doesn't happen to your exact specifications. Focus on expecting the generalities of your goals. Leave the rest up to the universe, *and turn your disappointment into delight!*

Saturday

The words you speak are just as important as the words you think. Ensure that when you're talking out loud, you're speaking of all the good that is coming and happening to you. Not only will it reaffirm *your position, but it will* attract *even more!*

Sunday

One of the greatest joys in life is sharing unconditionally, but our monkey mind tends to trick us into sharing for gain. Challenge yourself today by doing things for others without expecting something in return,

reveling in the feeling of do-gooding for no other reason than to do good. It makes the world go 'round.

When you're feeling low, it's always nice to get a little pick-me-up from someone you adore and admire—and it's just as nice to return the favor, whether those you adore are low or not.

Tell someone—or everyone—you care for something about them that you enjoy. It'll make everyone feel good, and feeling good is what it's all about.

Monday

Tuesday

Manifesting your life is a process, and one that requires you to keep moving forward. Take a look at where you might be stuck in a cycle that you need to break out of, then find the courage to break free. It's tough, but *rewarding* in the end.

ARE YOU A GLASS HALF EMPTY KIND OF PERSON?

It's time to look at the glass half full. Instead of falling into the temptation of a shame spiral, find the bright side of everything. Not only will it make you feel better, but problems won't seem so insurmountable anymore.

Thursday

Anyone can be psychic to a certain degree—
it's just a matter of taking a moment to think before you act.
Take a look at how you handle certain situations today, paying close attention to your emotional state when you're confronted with things. That's what will help you learn what the outcome of the situation will be.

When you think of, work for and accept only the best, guess what happens? Only the best comes to you! If you're feeling as though you're lacking in any of these areas, figure out how to make one or all of them the absolute best you can. Your life is waiting!

If your manifestations are seeming more like "maybes," then maybe you need to solidify your dreams and really root into what it is you want. Remember—the universe only acts when you believe it to be yours.

Remember that when you do actions that affect you, your actions also affect the whole universe. How are you affecting yourself today? Take note and act according to what brings your manifestations ever closer.

Allowing yourself to be sucked into jealousy just serves to cut you off from your own potential. Celebrate your neighbor's achievements not just to encourage your own, but to spread joy around the universe. What you put out there comes back to you tenfold.

When you try to lock down the hows, whys and wheres, all you do is cut yourself off from the absolute best outcome that could happen. Leave your options open—it's the best way for everything to come to you in a way even

Tuesday

better than you imagined.

Wednesday

If life seems complicated, it's usually because we're doing something to complicate it. Take a moment to figure out some way to uncomplicate things for yourself, whether it be figuring out an easier route to work or wearing something else. Little changes can make all the difference.

Your instinct is the most powerful tool you can use to guide you, and yet most of us squash it when we hear it kick in. Tune in today and see what your instinct tells you, where it leads you, and how you respond to it. It might just bring you one step closer to where you want to be.

The state of your mind is in direct correlation to the state of your body.
Are you fit as a fiddle, or in agonizing pain?

Friday

A simple walking regimen can get both your mind and body on track and in sync,
so try taking a spin around the block today.
It can open up your world in ways you wouldn't expect.

Feeling happy isn't enough—you need to be happy with every fiber of your being! Explore new ways to live in happiness today, whether it be running through a field of flowers, jumping in the ocean naked, painting or sculpting or singing your lungs out.

Saturday

Do it all the way!

It's not about having luck so much as creating it, and how much you have depends on how much you create. Want to know how? Listening to your intuition, paying attention to the signs, thinking before you act…

Sunday

all these things will increase your chances of good luck.
Find new ways to make luck for yourself today.

Life is ever changing.

You are ever changing.

You are not what you used to be.

What was that plant before it was here?

It was a seed.

What will it be when it changes to something else?

It will leave its seeds behind and

grow more of itself.

You can grow just this way.

Think to the Universe.

Ask to grow.

Ask for what you need.

Believe you will be ever-changing like the plant.

Notes

Even when it seems like there's nothing happening for you, the universe has about a million different things it's doing, trying and working on to make things go in your direction. When it feels like things are stagnant, play a game in your mind where you see all the puzzle pieces fit into place…then watch as it becomes so.

Tuesday

*Starting with a certain and definite dream is the first part of attaining it,
but the second part is taking a step into the uncertain and indefinite.*
Let go of your fear and see where your feet lead you.

When your mind starts clinging to the mistakes of the past,

Wednesday

sit for a moment with the feeling it brings up in you, then tell that feeling that it no longer serves you and it's time to go. Literally—say it out loud! Setting your intention will make it so, and make more room for good thoughts to flood you.

Thursday

Don't forget that you always have options, even when it seems like you don't. You can always change that job, leave that city, end that relationship. Or you can change your perspective on all those things and watch them become something completely different. It's always up to you.

You may not have control over a situation, but you always have control
over how you react to it. When faced with adversity, do you blow up or
do you handle things calmly and gracefully?
Guess which way encourages the path you want to be on, versus the path you're on?

Saturday

It's so **tempting to criticize others** *for their shortcomings, wrongdoings and misdeeds, but you only judge others as you judge yourself. Instead of judging others, take a look in the mirror and determine what it is inside you that is festering, angering you or needs fixing.*

It's not as hard as you think.

N. Y.

Have you ever heard someone say, "They're looking for trouble?" *Has someone said it to* *you? Examine ways in which you look for trouble, whether you* willingly *walk down a dark* *alleyway or look for an opportunity to fight, then* teach *yourself to turn the other way. Trouble* *is an old habit that's great to break.*

The easiest way to bring yourself up when you're feeling down is to treat yourself as the king or queen you really are. On days when you feel tempted to schlub around, challenge yourself and primp, prime, and dress up! You'll be amazed at how it transforms your mood.

The closer you get to attaining and achieving your goals, the more likely it is you'll want to backslide into old behavior patterns, be it focusing on the negative, fighting with people, road rage, what have you. Find ways to stop yourself from going down that path and focus on staying on the right one. It's never easy, but nothing worth having is.

Wednesday

Want comes from desire, need comes from lack.
*Today, address your wants versus your needs…and discover new ways
to turn your needs into wants.*

Thursday

If your life is chaotic to an uncontrollable degree, find places where you can create pockets of peace. Drive in silence, create a meditation space in your home, find a way to get away, even if it's just for five minutes. It will make a world of difference to your mental health.

But on the flip side,

Friday

too much escaping isn't good for you, either. Only you know whether your escapes are running away or taking a time out, so ensure that you're conscious of which is which. Deal with the things you're trying to escape while you take time out for yourself to ensure mole hills don't become mountains.

Saturday

One of the best ways to change your perspective on life is to take yourself out of your comfort zone, whether that means traveling to a far-off land or just to your local soup kitchen to volunteer.

Unlocking your patterns can unlock powerful things from inside you.

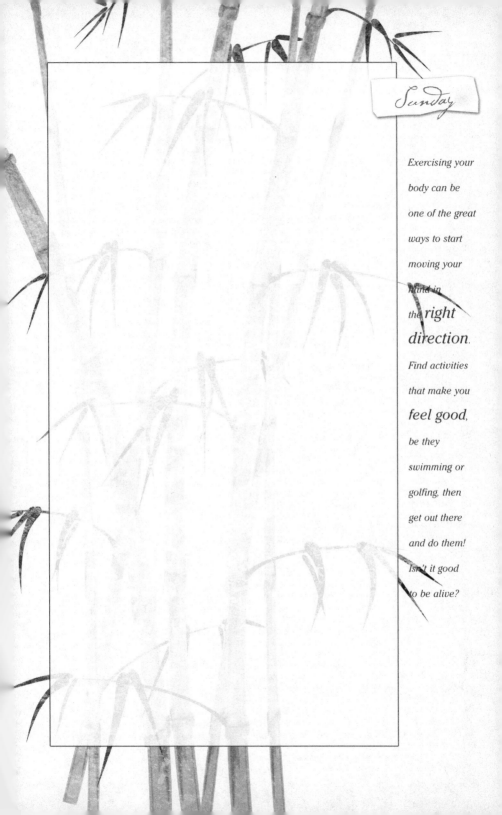

Sunday

Exercising your
body can be
one of the great
ways to start
moving your
mind in
the **right**
direction.
Find activities
that make you
feel good,
be they
swimming or
golfing, then
get out there
and do them!
Isn't it good
to be alive?

Before you do anything this morning, grab a pen and write down five things you'd like to see happen today—and remember, they have to be believable for you. At the end of the day, go back to your list and see how many come true. Try doing this for the week, the month, the year…and soon you'll know how to script your life!

Tuesday

*You never have to worry about your dreams outshining someone else's—
there's enough abundance for everyone. But if you're truly worried about it, share
what you have with others.* **What goes around comes around!**

A *belief* is only a thought you keep thinking, so shouldn't you keep thinking about the things you believe?

Taking a cyclical, *reaffirming approach* to your wants and desires only solidifies them. Let your mind obsess just a little!

When you
spend so much
time thinking,
dreaming and
manifesting
all the things
you want,
sometimes
your brain can
tire from all
the work.

Take some
time out
today to let
your mind
wander and
see where it
goes. You
might be sur-
prised at
what you
discover!

Thursday

Friday

Is there someone in your life that's driving you crazy?
Don't focus on what makes you mad about them, focus on what's good about them.
Taking a simple shift in perspective can change your whole outlook
on people and how you deal with them, making life that much easier.

Saturday

EVERYTHING IS POSSIBLE,

it's just a matter of what you wish to turn into possibility! Do you allow yourself to consider all your thoughts and dreams, or do you reign yourself in? Unleash the power of your mind today and revel in what comes forth!

Sunday

When something is uncomfortable, it's because we're seeing, doing or experiencing
something that encourages us to grow—and that's good! A flower has to struggle to move

from seed to blossom,

and so shall you as you manifest your desires. Today, revel in the struggle and
explore ways to make it easier on yourself without shying away from the process.

Remember that what you focus on becomes your reality. So if you're constantly focused on not having any money, guess what? You won't have any. But if you choose to focus on getting more work so that more money will come in, suddenly your bills will take care of themselves. Try shifting your attention to the solution rather than the problem, and watch how much easier life becomes to navigate.

Bringing your life into balance can be a challenge,

but identifying what you do to throw it out of balance is the majority of the battle. Do you push yourself when you know you should rest? Do you eat something when you know it makes you sick? Show a little compassion for yourself. It'll bring that life balance ever closer.

Your body is a product of your thoughts. Not feeling well? Chances are you're not thinking well, either. When you're starting to feel run down, examine the things running through your mind and work on affirming your health instead of welcoming the sickness.

Wednesday

You need your strength to manifest your dreams.

Thursday

*Nothing fails…unless you look
at something as a failure. Resist
the urge to label something that
has happened in your life as a
failure—look at it as a lesson
learned instead. It's just another
way to affirm the positive.*

"If my mind can conceive it, and my heart can believe it, I know I can achieve it."
—Jesse Jackson

*Living and being
it will bring it!*

Disease is just the body's way of telling you that it's out of balance and needs attention. Treating the symptom will work for a little while, but getting to the cause will solve the problem for sure. **Be creative in how you deal with your health, and don't lose hope.**

Anxiety feels real, but it's just a product of the negativity in your mind. The next time you feel yourself getting anxious, stop and think about what's really causing you to spin out of control. Address the problem, and if there's something that can be done, do it. If not, let it go. Worrying will just make you ill.

We often take for granted how our body has the ability to heal itself. Think of what happens when you scrape your knee or battle a bacterial infection. Today, explore the ways that your body can heal itself. You never know until you try.

Monday

When you feel yourself going into a corner of your mind that seems scary, don't shy away and turn tail—move toward it. The resistance you feel is just habit, but unlocking that door will give you freedom beyond your wildest dreams.

When you're perpetually focused on the bad, the not having, the things that are wrong with life, you're just solidifying them in your consciousness. Challenge yourself to see the other side of the coin, and see what it brings up for you.

Wednesday

Sow a thought,

and you reap an act;

Sow an act,

and you reap a habit;

Sow a habit,

and you reap a character;

Sow a character,

and you reap a destiny."

Charles Reade

Thursday

Happier thoughts lead to happier biochemistry, which leads to a happier body. What do you think about when you look at your body? Change your thought process, and your body will change, too.

Friday

Do you love yourself unconditionally?

You live with yourself 24 hours a day, 7 days a week…(shouldn't you?) Find the things you don't love about yourself, and discover a way to love them. When you love yourself, everyone else will, too.

As the saying goes, "Man becomes what he thinks about." Take a moment to look at what you are today, and decide if it fits with your goals and dreams. Reaffirm the things that do, rethink the things that don't.

Saturday

Only you have the power to change.

When you think about what you want, you give energy. When you think about what you don't want, often you give even more energy to that than what you do want in an effort to avoid it...but that only draws it ever nearer. Don't fight against something, flow with the antithesis of it instead.

Does it make sense to give a problem more energy than the solution? That will only create more problems. Once you've identified the issue, let it go and start looking for the solution. Dwelling on the problem only makes it solidify.

When someone asks you how things are going, even if they're not,
tell them "Things are great!" Why? Because the more you say it,
the more you'll reinforce it in your mind. And then things really will be great.

Tuesday

Energy flows where attention goes, so where do you want
to go today? Before you get out of bed, try manifesting
your day in your head. See what you can
create. With practice, every day will become **a joy**.

N. Y.

Don't try to change the world and the people around you—that will just leave you frustrated and exhausted, which cuts you off from the flow of the universe. Find the joy in everyone and everything instead. Going with the flow is what it's all about.

Friday

The more you think there won't be enough, the more you bring it into reality. Discover ways to trick your mind into havingness instead of fear and dread. Beautiful things will unfold as a result.

Saturday

Limitations are all in your mind,
so it's time to look at what's putting them there. What are you afraid of? Do you think you're not good enough? Once you address the root of your limitations, you can break free of them.

There's more than enough good to go around because there's more than enough creativity and mind power to make it go around. Try stretching the recesses of your brain to see how creative you can become in your manifestations. Flex those muscles!

The power of your
mind is infinite,

Monday

so why shouldn't your manifestations be? Ensure that your dreams are continual, evolving and everlasting by updating your vision board, continuing to create your day, and embracing all that it brings.

Tuesday

Life is meant to be abundant,

which is why you often find solutions for issues when you think you've done all you can.
How else can life be abundant for you? Look at all the possibilities today, and when
you think you've seen them all, look again.

Wednesday

When you feel
as though you
are lacking, often
times it's because
you're **not
opening** your
eyes to all the
possibilities.
Find a quiet
space to
meditate on
what you
need help with,
and watch the
answers come
to you. It's just
that simple.

Do you live through your heart or your mind?

Certainly you want to use your mind to create your world, but you need the passion of your heart to enjoy it and make it come true. Find ways for your heart to overpower your mind from time to time and watch a more enriching life unfold.

Friday

*Not everyone **wants the same** thing you do, nor do you want the same thing everyone else does. The next time you find yourself concerned with the universe's ability to produce for you, recall that you're a unique being, and your wants and needs are just **as unique**. There is enough for everyone.*

Saturday

If you believe it, you will see it.

If you act from it, it will appear for you. Look at the ways you are believing,
seeing and acting today—it will tell you why you are where you are,
and how you can get to where you want to be.

All the bliss, joy, love, abundance, prosperity, wonderment and amazement is there waiting for you to grab hold of it...so why haven't you?

Is there something holding you back? Find out what it is, and break through that wall today!

Sunday

Monday

Are you **intentional, passionate**, and **on fire** for what you want?
If so, live it and breathe it! If not, find something that makes you feel that way!
You hold the **power to live** the life you want in your mind, heart and hand.

Blessing and praising the beautiful and wonderful things around you only serves to bring more blessings, more beautiful and wonderful things. Who doesn't want that? Find new ways to bless and praise the good around you, and watch more good unfold.

Wednesday

If there are things that aren't working the way you want them to, don't waste time and energy complaining—use all that passion instead to go after what you do want in your life.

That's the way to turn things around.

Thursday

When your life starts to turn around and you feel the joy that comes along with what you're experiencing, don't hold back—share it with others. Encourage them to do the same with their lives that you did with yours. It just serves to keep the positivity going.

to feel like the bad things that are happening to you are just things that happen to you and you alone, stop and realize that you are but one small part of a huge, wide, vast universe…and that it's ever-changing and ever-evolving—and always takes care of you. Just make sure you're taking care of it, too.

You are an infinite field of possibilities, but are you living like it? Are you wandering through life with your eyes open? Open your eyes in a new way, looking at things as if it were the first time you're seeing them. You never know what you might discover.

Saturday

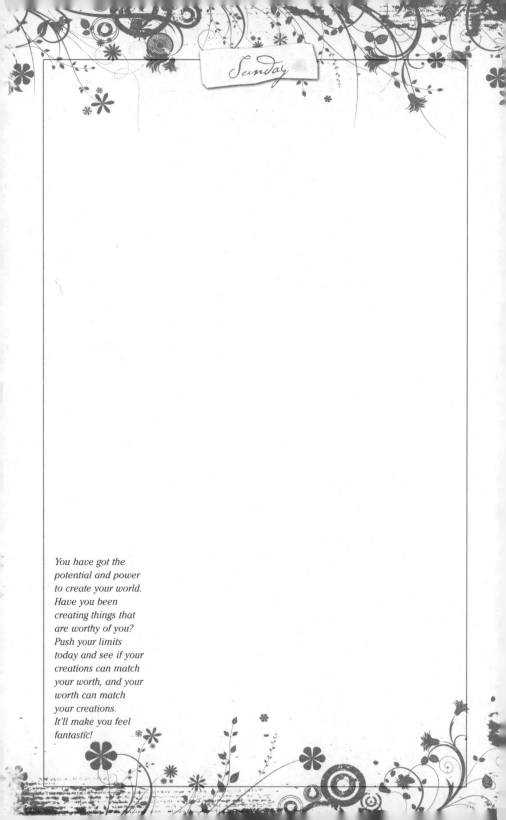

Sunday

You have got the
potential and power
to create your world.
Have you been
creating things that
are worthy of you?
Push your limits
today and see if your
creations can match
your worth, and your
worth can match
your creations.
It'll make you feel
fantastic!

You are not a victim in life. Sure, bad things happen to good people, but it's what you do with it that counts. Find ways to let go of what was and what used to be while making lemonade out of lemons.

Monday

The infinite opens up when you do.

*The question is, what do you choose now? Despite your past,
who you were, who's hurt you and what you experienced yesterday,
what do you want today? Make a list. Read it aloud.*

Start solidifying it today.

Have you ever felt like someone is having fun with your life at your expense? Put a stop to it!
Literally put a pen in your hand and change the ending! Write out what you'd rather a situation turn
into instead of what it is, and believe it to be true. You can change your life!

*The one thing you need to remember is that life is fluid. Just because
your life is one way today doesn't mean you can't change it tomorrow.*

Thursday

*Your purpose is what you say it is. Find one thing today that you'd
really like to have change, then focus on the solution for changing it.*

If you don't enjoy what you're doing, why do it? All that does is send those "feel bad" vibrations out into the universe, which causes it to respond in kind. Stop doing what you don't enjoy and find something you do enjoy instead!

Friday

Notes

"Men are not prisoners of fate,
but only prisoners of their own mind."

Franklin D. Roosevelt

They say that laughter is the greatest medicine, and they're right! Make sure you find some way to laugh and enjoy life every day, even if it's just a little giggle here, a snicker there. Watch things change as a result!

Saturday

Sunday

Inner happiness is the fuel of success, but are you happy on the inside? It's easy to fake it to others, not so to fake it to yourself. Find ways to make yourself happy today, and bask in the feeling of doing it. It will bring more good to you.

Monday

It's all a matter of following your bliss. Once you do, walls will crumble, doors will open, the universe will do everything in its power to bring it to you. Identify what makes you the most blissful today.

Feel it, live it, breathe it, be it.

Exercise is a simple yet wonderful way to help clear old energy blocks from the past, but the key is not losing yourself in mindlessness while you do it.

Tuesday

Take a hike through nature, try doing some yoga, do something that takes you out of your element and comfort zone while keeping you within yourself.

Wednesday

Remember that, at most, we use 5% of the human mind. As you go about your day, explore ways to expand your mind past its usual experiences, beliefs, thoughts. It's a great way to expand your possibilities and the universe around you.

Can you see yourself with the life that you desire? Close your eyes and play a movie in your mind of you experiencing, feeling, tasting all the wonderment that your heart desires. Seeing it—even in your mind—helps you believe it.

What you see is only the tip of the iceberg, it's also about what **you know, understand and believe**. *Today, take a moment to understand what you know, understand and believe about your desires.* *That's when you'll see them.*

Saturday

When you think **it's not possible**, *read up on people who did impossible things like walking on the moon, changing the face of music as we know it, building and creating things that seemed unreal as they were happening. It will change your mind about what you're truly capable of.*

All you are and all you ever were is a vibrating mass of energy. Thoughts have frequencies, so when you're thinking great things, you're vibrating at a high frequency. Thinking about bad things makes you vibrate at a lower level. Feel where you're vibrating today, and discover ways to up your frequency.

Monday

You can't escape the Law of Attraction, no matter how much you try. Everything in your life is something you've drawn to you. If you've drawn something bad or unsavory, be patient—the good can sometimes be obstructed by the bad, but it's always there.

Tuesday

How do you move from a negative vibration into a positive one?

Do something that makes you happy, think about something that brings you joy,
listen to music that gets your toe tapping…do whatever you have to do to distract
your mind from the negativity it clings to. It works.

Wednesday

You have the conscious ability to choose the images you will see in your mind, which is how you create your reality. What are the images you see in your mind? Take stock, and discard the ones that don't work in harmony with what you want.

Because you're a sensitive,

Thursday

energetic being, sometimes you have the ability to pick up other people's thoughts—and that can get confusing! When you find yourself thinking something that doesn't seem in tune with you, determine if it might be from someone else. Then, send that thought back to its rightful owner. You need to focus on yourself!

Friday

Do you see what you want coming into your life, or do you find it hard to picture?
Try this simple trick—visualize what you want happening to someone close to you, then ease
yourself in the picture until you're the sole beneficiary of all the abundance you seek.

Before you know it, you'll be living it!

Saturday

Saying "That will never happen to me" ensures that it never will. Try saying, **"It's going to happen to me!"** That's what will ensure *it will!*

You become what you think about.

You have the freedom to think about what you want, and you also have the freedom to pick which thoughts you want. Make sure you pick the good ones today!

Monday

The universe is *infinite*, so if you find yourself worrying about taking more than your share, that's your self-doubt throwing in obstacles. *Find creative ways* to distract it while you work on manifesting your goals. Quieting your monkey mind will make it easier for all you desire to come to you.

If you *want more* wealth, greater health, a better relationship,
find the image in your mind right now, then make sure
it's on your vision board.

See it in your mind and see it on your board.
Bombard yourself at every turn. It will help make it all the more real.

The good that you want is already here— all you have to do is get in harmony with it, and the easiest way to do that is with your thinking. Seek out different ways to tune your thoughts into what you want instead of what you don't, whether that means watching movies that emulate your goals, reading about people whose lives you admire, or spending time with those who have achieved things you want to achieve.

Wednesday

The world is the way you want to see it, and so is your life. When you look at your life, what do you see? Your immediate answer to that question will tell you everything you need to know about where your mind is at, and what, if anything, you need to change to get on track.

Friday

Changing your habitual way of thinking seems like it's easier said than done, but it's not as complicated as you think. It's all about being aware. Pay attention to your dreams and what they tell you, let your emotions be your guide, and continue to do things that make you happy. Soon everything will fall in sync.

You never know what will help you establish your life's purpose until you expand your horizons outside of what you're used to. Take a trip to your local bookstore and see what strikes your fancy.

The answers could lay inside those pages.

Do you believe in yourself? It's time to make sure that you do. Find ways to bask in your own glory and build up your own self-esteem by teaching yourself new things. Knowledge is power.

Monday

the more your belief about it will change. Today, take a look at a situation in your life that's been on your mind—be it bad or good—and roll it around in your brain, looking for all the angles and possibilities. Not only will your beliefs about it change, but an answer you're looking for might just appear.

It's time to reevaluate the laws that govern your being and determine which are in harmony with who and what you are right now. Are the ways you govern yourself based on who you were, or who you are? Figure out which is which, and filter accordingly.

Wednesday

The fact of the matter is, you're created in the likeness of the universe. You are all it is, all it was, and all it will ever be. The sooner you understand that, the sooner you realize how in control you are of your life. Discover new ways to celebrate your infinite wonderment today…and start the whole process over again tomorrow.

Today, understand this one principle: you are as important as anyone who has ever lived. The only difference between those who have been successful with fame, wealth, etc., and you, is that they tapped into the unlimited supply that the universe offered. With good habits, you can do this, too.

Thursday

Friday

Think for five minutes about the things you are best at doing in life.
Focus on those things for the rest of the day.
You will find more of this hidden treasure within you.

Saturday

Become a mentor to somebody. Understand that this positive impact is money in the universe bank.

Celebrate every little achievement, whether this is getting your kids to school on time, matching all your socks coming out of the washing machine, or getting a salary raise.

Sunday

Today is a day for celebration.

"The purpose of life, after all, is to live it, to taste experience to the utmost, to reach out eagerly and without fear for newer and richer experiences."

—*Eleanor Roosevelt*

Monday

"We must be the change we
wish to see in the world."

Gandhi